Technology through the Ages

WARFARE
THROUGH THE AGES
From Bows to Bombs

MICHAEL WOODS AND MARY B. WOODS

TWENTY-FIRST CENTURY BOOKS / MINNEAPOLIS

For Violet Woods-Powers

Twenty-First Century Books™
An imprint of Lerner Publishing Group, Inc.
241 First Avenue North
Minneapolis, MN 55401 USA

For reading levels and more information, look up this title at www.lernerbooks.com.

Main body text set in Bembo Std Regular.
Typeface provided by Monotype Typography.

Library of Congress Cataloging-in-Publication Data

Names: Woods, Mary B. (Mary Boyle), 1946–author. | Woods, Michael, 1946–author.
Title: Warfare through the ages : from bows to bombs / Michael Woods and Mary B. Woods.
Description: Minneapolis, MN : Twenty–First Century Books, 2025. | Series: Technology through the ages | Audience: Ages 11–18 | Audience: Grades 7–9 | Summary: "From the first spear throwers to the dreaded Claws of Archimedes, discover the ancient technologies that changed the course of human history"—Provided by publisher.
Identifiers: LCCN 2023037045 (print) | LCCN 2023037046 (ebook) | ISBN 9798765610077 (library binding) | ISBN 9798765629932 (paperback) | ISBN 9798765639016 (epub)
Subjects: LCSH: Military art and science—History—To 500—Juvenile literature. | Military history, Ancient—Juvenile literature. | Weapons, Ancient—Juvenile literature. | Military weapons—Juvenile literature.
Classification: LCC U29 .W597 2025 (print) | LCC U29 (ebook) | DDC 355/.0209—dc23/eng/20231107

LC record available at https://lccn.loc.gov/2023037045
LC ebook record available at https://lccn.loc.gov/2023037046

Manufactured in the United States of America
1 – CG – 7/15/24

CONTENTS

INTRODUCTION

W hat do you think of when you hear the word *technology*? You probably think of something totally new. You might think of computers, powerful microscopes, and other scientific tools. But technology isn't just brand-new machines and discoveries. Technology is as old as human society.

Technology is the use of knowledge and inventions to make human life better. *Technology* comes from Greek. *Tekhne* means "art" or "craft." Adding the suffix *-logia* meant "the study of arts and crafts." In modern times, the word usually refers to a craft, a technique, or a tool.

People use many kinds of technology. Medicine, transportation, and agriculture are all kinds of technologies. This book looks at a form of technology that has helped people survive enemy attacks and expand their political, social, and economic influence: military technology, or warfare.

Assyrian warriors attack an enemy village in this relief carving from the palace of King Tiglath-Pileser III, who ruled what is now northern Iraq from 745 to 727 BCE.. Civilizations that held the advantage in warfare technology could conquer vast empires.

Learning about Ancient Warfare

Ancient weapons were simple. Most ancient soldiers fought with spears, daggers, and bows and arrows. Yet these simple weapons could be very destructive. In ancient wars, tens of thousands of men might die in a single battle. Sometimes ancient armies destroyed whole cities and conquered entire empires.

Ancient people left us a lot of information about armies, battles, and weapons. Many ancient writers recorded military history. Ancient artists often made sculptures and drawings of warriors. Some ancient weapons were made of wood, animal bone, or other natural materials that decayed long ago. Others were made of stone or metal. Modern scholars can study these weapons and the remains of ancient military structures to learn how, when, and where they were used.

Sometimes it takes a little digging to find out about ancient technology. Around the world, ancient peoples built houses, storage sheds, and military forts, but these structures didn't always last. War, earthquakes, or storms damaged some buildings. Other buildings simply fell. People often hauled away the old wood, brick, or stone and constructed new buildings where the old ones had stood. Only the foundations from the original buildings remained.

Some people abandoned their settlements for places that had more food or that were easier to defend. Their old houses and other buildings eventually collapsed. Winds blew dirt into the structures. Rainstorms filled them with more dirt and mud. Plants grew over the new layers of earth. Houses and even whole ancient towns were buried and forgotten.

That's where archaeologists come in. These scientists study the remains of past cultures. Often they have to dig through layers of earth to find traces of ancient structures. Sometimes they unearth entire ancient buildings. More often, only portions of the buildings remain. At dig sites, archaeologists often find the remains of ancient military technology. They find ancient weapons, armor, and defensive walls. Read on and discover how ancient warriors fought and changed the course of history.

CHAPTER ONE

Warfare Basics

The first *Homo sapiens*, or modern humans, lived about three hundred thousand years ago. They lived in small groups and got their food by hunting game, fishing, and gathering wild plants. When the food in one area was used up, the group moved to a new place. Hunter-gatherers made tools from stone, wood, animal bones, plant fibers, and clay. In some places, the hunter-gatherer lifestyle has remained unchanged.

Sticks and Stones

Early humans made knives and axes by knocking rocks together. They used one rock to break flakes off another, leaving the second stone with a sharp edge. Early humans made spears from long straight sticks with stone spearheads attached to the end. They made clubs from wood and animal bone. People used these tools to hunt animals.

Archaeologists think that early humans probably used their hunting weapons during these battles over food or land.

This wall carving from a palace at Nineveh (near modern-day Mosul, Iraq) shows soldiers in battle armed with slings, ready to launch deadly projectiles. The relief dates to around 700 BCE.

New Technology

As the centuries passed, ancient peoples developed new hunting tools. One was the spear-thrower. This device was a simple stick, a little shorter than a person's arm. The front end of the spear-thrower rested in a hunter's hand. The spear rested on top of the spear thrower. When the hunter released the spear, the back end of the spear-thrower pushed the spear forward with extra force. With a spear-thrower, a hunter could propel a spear four times farther than with muscle power alone. The oldest known spear-throwers come from

caves in France. They date to around 15,000 to 11,000 BCE.

Like spear-throwers, slings allowed ancient hunters to launch missiles with more force than they could with only muscle power. Slings used stones as the missile. When fired from a sling, a small stone could be deadly. A sling was made from two leather cords fastened to a leather pouch. The hunter put a small stone in the pouch, held both cords, and whirled the device overhead to give the stone momentum. At just the right instant, he released one of the cords. The stone shot toward its target.

Another simple hunting tool was the throwing stick. This weapon was just a stick thrown through the air. Unlike spears, which flew straight, throwing sticks spun end over end in flight. A well-thrown stick could kill a rabbit, a bird, or another small animal. Most throwing sticks were made of wood, but hunters also made them from animal bones and tusks.

Eventually hunters discovered that flat, curved throwing sticks flew farther than round, straight ones. They hit their targets with more force. Their winglike design helped the sticks stay aloft. Hunters began to fashion boomerangs. Most people associate boomerangs with Australia. They are used by some Aboriginal Australians, and the name *boomerang* comes from Australia. But ancient peoples in other parts of the world also used boomerangs.

Spear-throwers, slings, throwing sticks, and boomerangs all made hunting easier and more efficient. And once people had learned to kill animals with these tools, they realized they could use them against human enemies. A cave painting from northern Australia shows what might be the first-ever battle scene. The painting shows warriors holding spears,

Magic Paintings

Boomerangs come in two types: returning and non-returning. Both types are curved, flat sticks. But returning boomerangs have a sharper, more V-shaped curve. This special shape allows returning boomerangs to fly through the air and return to the spot from which they were thrown. Ancient Australians invented returning boomerangs. In flight they looked like birds of prey. Australian hunters used them to frighten or trick game birds.

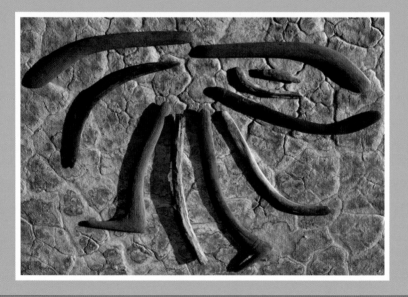

boomerangs, and clubs. Some of the soldiers stoop to help injured comrades, who have spears sticking out of their bodies. The painting is more than ten thousand years old, but ancient peoples may have been fighting with one another thousands of years before that.

Ancient Archers

We do not know who invented the bow and arrow or when. But the invention was a breakthrough in both ancient hunting and ancient warfare technologies. Early hunters made bows from pieces of flexible wood, such as elm, ash, or yew. They made a bowstring from animal intestines, flax, or another fiber. The bowstring connected one end of the bow to the other. It pulled the two ends of the bow toward each other, so the bow was slightly curved.

To use the weapon, an archer held the bow in one hand. He attached an arrow to the bowstring and drew

This relief from the eighth century BCE shows ancient Assyrian archers besieging a city.

back the bowstring with the other hand. The archer's pull increased the bend of the bow. When the archer let go of the bowstring, the bow sprung back to its original shape. This quick unbending of the bow propelled the arrow forward.

The first arrows were made from strong reeds or tree branches. Finding the right branch was important, because only a perfectly straight arrow would fly straight. Arrows were usually about half the length of bows. The weight of an arrow was also important. A light arrow would fly the farthest but had less power to pierce its target. A heavy arrow had great power but would not fly very far.

At first, arrow makers simply sharpened one end of an arrow into a point. The other end was notched, or cut with a thin indentation, to fit the bowstring. Later, arrow makers learned to harden the points of arrows by heating them in a fire. Then hunters realized that an arrowhead made of a sharp piece of stone would help the arrow cut and pierce its target. Arrows with good arrowheads pierced flesh deeply and killed quickly. With arrowheads, the bow and arrow was the world's most deadly weapon for thousands of years.

CHAPTER TWO

The Ancient Middle East

Around 10,000 BCE, people in the Middle East began to abandon the hunter-gatherer lifestyle. In a region called the Fertile Crescent, they began to raise crops and livestock. They settled into farming villages. Early farmers grew enough food for their families and sometimes even more food than they needed. When they had a surplus, they could sell or trade it. This surplus of food let some people specialize in jobs other than farming, allowing more complex societies to develop. These complex societies created laws and governments to organize and control the people. Rulers who controlled the land that food was grown on wanted to protect their territory. They often wanted more territory, wealth, and power. They needed weapons and armies.

Ancient Draft

Amassing a large army has never been easy. Many people don't want to join the army. After all, that job can get you hurt or killed. To solve this problem, many governments require

This limestone carving from Abu Simbel in southern Egypt dates to the thirteenth century BCE. The picture shows Hittite soldiers, who carry large, round shields for protection.

people—especially young men—to join the army. The system of calling up people for military service is called a draft. Many ancient kingdoms drafted people into the army.

In the ancient kingdom of Mari, in modern-day Syria, the government required men to serve in the military. They were supposed to register for service at government offices. But despite the offer of free meals and gifts, many men refused to register. The officer in charge of registration proposed a solution to Zimri-Lim, Mari's king: "If my lord will agree, let me execute a criminal [a man who had refused to register] in the prison, cut off his head and parade it all around the town . . . to make men afraid so that they will assemble quickly."

We don't know if Zimri-Lim agreed to the idea. But we do know that he was a successful military leader who never lacked troops.

Enough to Feed an Army

Imagine trying to feed an ancient army of one hundred thousand soldiers every day. Ancient soldiers were hungry people, who sometimes marched or fought all day. How could ancient armies get the food they needed?

Armies transported some food in wheeled carts. They also took along self-transporting food in the form of herds of cattle. The cattle marched with the army. They grazed on grass along the way. Soldiers killed cows and ate them as needed. But soldiers still needed more food.

To solve the problem, ancient Middle Eastern armies would steal food from farms and villages along their route. As soldiers marched, they picked crops, took livestock, and raided stockpiles of grain, beer, wine, olive oil, and other foods belonging to local people. The strategy of feeding soldiers off the land had a terrible effect on civilians. They often starved after an army marched past.

Made of Metal

The first weapons were made from natural materials. These included rocks, bones, and sticks. Around 5000 BCE, people in the ancient Middle East began making weapons and other tools from copper. Copper is a soft metal found underground. By heating and hammering copper, ancient craftspeople could easily shape it into swords, arrowheads, and other weapons.

Around 3000 BCE, Middle Eastern metalsmiths learned to make a harder metal. They melted copper and tin together in a hot furnace, then let the mixture cool and harden. The result was bronze. Bronze weapons did not bend or break as easily as copper ones. Copper blades often grew dull after repeated use. Bronze blades stayed sharp longer.

In about 1550 BCE, invaders from modern-day Turkey marched toward Mesopotamia, a region between the Tigris and Euphrates Rivers in modern-day Iraq. These invaders were the Hittites. Other Middle Eastern groups feared them, and they quickly conquered Mesopotamia. The Hittites' power rested in their strong weapons and armor. These weapons were made of iron. Iron weapons were stronger than the bronze used by other groups. An iron sword could cut a bronze sword in half. The Hittites may have made their first iron by melting meteorites. These pieces of rock-like material fall to Earth from space. Later, however, the Hittites learned to smelt iron from ore dug out of the ground. They heated the ore with charcoal and other materials to melt the ore and separate out the iron. Although the Hittites tried to keep iron technology a secret, the information soon spread. Other groups began to make iron weapons, and the Hittites lost their military advantage.

War on Wheels

The earliest armies fought on foot. They marched until they neared the enemy. When they were within firing distance, archers shot at the enemy with bows and arrows. Other soldiers moved in with spears, daggers, battle-axes, and clubs for hand-to-hand combat.

This Assyrian relief from the 600s BCE shows war chariots in the bloody Battle of Til-Tuba in ancient Iraq. War chariots were light, open-wheeled vehicles pulled by horses. Charioteers drove the fast vehicles and protected themselves with shields.

The ancient war chariot usually had two wheels. It was pulled by horses. Two or three soldiers rode in a chariot. In a three-person chariot, one drove, one shot arrows, and one held a shield to protect the archer and the driver. Soldiers in horse-drawn chariots could circle enemy foot soldiers and attack them with a shower of arrows. Foot soldiers were helpless against such an attack. Chariots moved too fast and were often too far away for foot soldiers to make a counterattack.

After thinning the enemy ranks from a distance, charioteers would charge directly into the enemy army. This tactic usually scattered the enemy soldiers. The charioteers could continue their attack while their army's foot soldiers moved in from another direction to further disrupt enemy defenses.

Before the introduction of chariots, military leaders who gathered the largest number of soldiers on a battlefield often won the battle. But chariots reduced the need for huge armies. Instead, the army with the most chariots and best-trained chariot crews had the edge.

Chariots did have disadvantages. They were expensive to build, and their crews required long training. Chariots were not effective in battles on rough or rocky land, which could injure horses and damage vehicles. One of their biggest drawbacks was the need for horses. Horses were expensive. In addition, they had to be fed and watered. Large horses may have needed 20 pounds (9kg) of hay and 8 gallons (30 liters) of water each day.

A Better Bow

Soon better bows were made. Instead of using a single strip of wood, they were made from two or more materials. This is called a composite, or collection, of materials.

A composite bow's interior layer was a strip of strong, flexible wood. The bow maker might glue a strip of animal horn along the inside curve of the bow. Strips of elastic, stretchy animal tendons were attached along the outer curve. The glue that held the materials together came from substances inside animal bone and hide.

Pulling on the bowstring of a composite bow stretched the sinew at the front of the bow and compressed the animal horn at the back. When the string was released, both materials instantly sprung back into shape. This combined springing motion propelled arrows toward their targets with great speed and force.

Composite bows were much more powerful than earlier bows. They could shoot arrows about two or three times farther. Composite bows were also shorter than earlier bows, so archers could easily fire them from the crowded interior of a chariot.

Horses Go to War

Horses in ancient times were smaller than the horses we know today. Most early horses were too small to ride in battle. But along with growing crops, early farmers also learned to breed animals. They mated male and female animals with desirable traits to produce offspring who also had those traits. For instance, the offspring of a large male horse and a large female horse would probably also be large. Over many centuries, horse breeders in Persia (modern-day Iran) and central Asia bred horses to be big, strong, and heavy. These new breeds were the first war horses.

But big horses weren't enough. For stability on horseback, ancient cavalry needed stirrups and saddles. Stirrups made horses easier to mount. Without stirrups, riders had to vault onto horses. That took a lot of strength and flexibility. Stirrups also added side-to-side balance. Saddles gave riders improved balance from front to back. With a stirrup and a saddle, the horse and rider became a single stable unit. With

Ancient cavalry (warriors on horseback) threw spears, shot arrows, and swung battle-axes while riding. Found in modern-day Iraq, this stone carving from the ancient palace of Ashurbanipal, king of the Assyrians in the 600s BCE, shows armed horsemen.

the rider's weight on the stirrups, a rider could carry a long spear, brace it firmly against their body, and charge an enemy. They could lift a heavy sword or battle-ax high above their head and slash down hard without losing balance. Many riders could even shoot arrows with great accuracy while galloping at full speed.

Archaeologists think that cavalry in central Asia were the first riders to use saddles. Ancient Indians were the first riders to use stirrups. Both kinds of technology then spread to the ancient Middle East.

On the Defensive

The development of more lethal offensive weapons created the need for better defensive warfare technology. This included armor, helmets, and shields. Soldiers of ancient Sumer (in modern-day Iraq) carried large rectangular shields. These protected the body from the neck to below the knees. A soldier held his shield with one hand and his weapon with the other. Shields were made of wood covered with layers of leather and cloth.

The first body armor was probably made of thick leather. Historians believe soldiers in Ur, an ancient Mesopotamian city, wore leather capes. The capes would have offered a layer of protection against minor cuts and body blows. But they probably weren't much help against heavy blows.

Assyrian soldiers wore tough leather garments that covered their bodies from chest to knees. Links of metal chain were sewn onto the leather. The metal provided protection against arrows and spears.

Soldiers in ancient Assyria wore cone-shaped hats. Made from cloth, leather, and metal, these were the first battle helmets. Because of the cone-shaped design, downward blows from a sword tended to glance off the helmets. A flap at the back of the helmet protected the soldier's neck.

City Walls

Most ancient cities were surrounded by high walls. The walls were built for defense. They had watchtowers, where defenders could keep a lookout for attackers. They also contained elevated platforms from which defenders could fire at attackers. In addition, many ancient cities were built on hills or other high ground. High ground is easier to defend than low ground. High ground offers a good view of approaching enemies. And it is much harder to scramble uphill to attack an enemy than to shoot or run downhill toward them.

While defenders did their best to keep ancient cities safe, attackers did their best to get past city walls. Attackers tried to climb over walls with the help of ropes and ladders. They tried to knock down city gates and walls by ramming them with heavy wooden beams. Sometimes they even attempted to tunnel under walls or burn through gates. Sometimes these tactics worked. Sometimes they didn't.

One tactic, first used in ancient Assyria, was superior to all others. It was called siege warfare. During a siege, soldiers

In this carving from ancient Iraq, dated to the mid-600s BCE, soldiers attack an enemy city using ladders, bows and arrows, and other weapons.

The Oldest Walled City

The first walled city known to archaeologists is Jericho, part of modern-day Israel. People built the city and its wall around 8000 BCE. The stone wall contained a brick watchtower, from which guards could look out for enemies. Guards climbed a spiral staircase to reach the top of the tower.

surrounded a walled town so that enemy soldiers and citizens could not leave or enter. The attackers cut off supplies of food and other materials that townspeople needed. They tried to starve the enemy until they surrendered. The attackers also tried to wear down the defenders with repeated attacks on the city walls. If the attackers were patient enough, they might not have to fight at all. They just had to wait outside the city until food and water ran out inside. Then the defenders would have to surrender or die.

But sieges were not usually that simple. If defenders had advance notice of an enemy's approach, they could prepare for a siege. Townspeople could stockpile food. They could bring cattle and sheep inside the city walls to provide a supply of milk and meat. In addition, most cities had wells within their walls to supply water. Sometimes such preparations worked. After weeks or months, the besieging army would get frustrated, grow short on food, and go home.

Guerrilla Warfare

Guerrilla warfare involves small bands of soldiers who make quick, small-scale ambushes. In conventional warfare, large armies meet on the battlefield. But guerrillas avoid such confrontations. Instead, they operate secretly and at night. They usually don't wear military uniforms, so enemies can't distinguish them from ordinary citizens.

Guerrilla warfare might sound like a modern technique. In fact, the term guerrilla, Spanish for "little war," wasn't coined until the early 1800s. But the ancient Scythians used guerrilla tactics more than twenty-five hundred years ago. The Scythians were nomads. They moved with herds of sheep, cattle, and horses around their home territory in modern-day Ukraine. In 513 BCE, Darius I, the king of Persia, invaded Scythian territory. Darius had the most powerful army in the world. But the Scythians resisted him by using guerrilla tactics. Small groups of Scythian cavalry approached Darius's army, but they never came near enough to fight. Instead, they retreated, luring Darius deeper and deeper into Scythian territory.

Ultimately, the guerrilla tactics worked. Darius realized he was losing too many soldiers to the Scythian's tactics and his army was running out of food. Darius retreated from Scythian territory. It never became part of his empire.

CHAPTER THREE

Ancient Egypt

Around 5000 BCE, ancient hunter-gatherers began to settle around the Nile River in Egypt. People built permanent farms and villages along the river. They grew wheat and other crops.

Eventually, two kingdoms developed in Egypt. Lower Egypt consisted of villages around the Nile delta. In this area the river splits into branches and empties into the Mediterranean Sea. Upper Egypt consisted of villages south of the Nile delta. Around 3100 BCE, Upper Egypt conquered Lower Egypt and the two kingdoms became one.

Sea Power

After uniting, Egypt became rich and powerful. The kingdom had fertile farmland, copper mines, and other natural resources. Egyptian rulers amassed large armies to protect the kingdom and to invade nearby countries.

Egypt also built a powerful navy. Shipbuilders constructed strong wooden warships. These vessels were sturdy enough

25

This wall painting from the Eighteenth Dynasty (1550–1292 BCE) shows an ancient Egyptian boat sailing the Nile. A sailor steers the ship with a big rudder located at the back, or stern, of the boat. Moving the rudder from side to side turns the boat to the left or the right.

to sail on the Mediterranean Sea. The warships used both wind power and people power. Each side of a ship had a row of oars, pulled by rowers. The ship also had a square sail attached to a mast. Sailors took advantage of wind power when traveling on the open sea. But for battle, they switched to human power. They lowered the sail and pulled down the ship's mast to protect it from damage. Then rowers powered the ship.

Egyptian warships were well designed for fighting. High gunwales, the edges around the sides of a ship, protected the rowers from enemy arrows. Raised platforms on the ship allowed archers to shoot their own arrows at the enemy. Some Egyptian warships had a ram on the front. Sailors used it to smash through the sides of enemy ships.

Hafting

Imagine an arrow with its head tied to the side of the shaft. The arrow would be unbalanced and would not fly straight. To work best, an arrowhead and its shaft need to be aligned directly end to end. Hafting is attaching the head or point of a weapon to a shaft. In the ancient world, maces, battle-axes, spears,

This carving from Luxor shows Pharaoh Ramses II firing an arrow from a bow.

arrows, and other weapons all needed to be hafted properly to work well.

Ancient craftspeople developed several hafting techniques. One was to put a tang, a small projecting tab, on the base of a spear or arrowhead. The tang fit into a slot at the end of the arrow or spear shaft. A cord tied tightly around the shaft constricted the slot. The tight slot held the tang in place.

Craftspeople used a similar technique to haft mace heads to handles. They drilled a hole into the stone mace head. They then pounded the handle firmly into the hole. The connection stayed tight, even after many swings.

The First Peace Treaty

Countries often end wars by signing peace treaties. These documents list the conditions under which all sides will stop fighting. The first written peace treaty that survives in full was written around 1270 BCE. In the treaty, the Egyptian ruler Ramses II and the Hittite king Hattusilis III agreed never to fight again. They agreed to send prisoners of war home and to help each other during future wars.

The Kadesh Peace Treaty was the first formal peace treaty in the modern world. The Hittite version of the treaty, pictured here, was carved on clay tablets. The Egyptian version was carved in hieroglyphics inside the walls of two temples in Egypt.

CHAPTER FOUR

Ancient China

People built the first villages in China around 3000 BCE. As Chinese society grew more complex, some groups began to fight among themselves for land and power.

Warfare in early China was similar to warfare in other ancient societies. Soldiers fought with spears, maces, and bows and arrows. They wore armor made from leather reinforced with metal. Some Chinese armor was made from tough rhinoceros skin. The Chinese even outfitted their horses with armor, which protected them from enemy spears and arrows.

The Chinese began using chariots in battle in the 1200s BCE. Generals used the vehicles as mobile command posts. The general rode in the chariot, along with a drummer, a driver, and archers. The archers defended the chariot with bows and arrows. As the chariot raced from place to place on the battlefield, the general gave orders to the drummer. Then the drummer pounded out signals on their drum. These signals directed troops on the battlefield.

This bronze figurine from ancient China shows a rider on a chariot. The Chinese used chariots in warfare as early as 1200 BCE.

The Crossbow

Around 400 BCE, the ancient Chinese invented the crossbow. This was the ancient world's most accurate long-range weapon. The ancient Chinese crossbow was similar to ordinary bows, but it was much more powerful. It was mounted horizontally on a frame. It had a crank or lever for drawing back the bowstring and arrow. An archer didn't have to pull on the string using muscle power alone. The crossbow also had a catch to hold the bowstring in place until the archer was ready to shoot. Bigger, stronger, and steadier than ordinary bows, crossbows could shoot

31

An illustration from the 1300s CE shows two Chinese warriors training with crossbows. Chinese soldiers used crossbows in battle for hundreds of years. Crossbows could shoot much farther than ordinary bows.

arrows farther and with more force. They could shoot accurately to about 1,320 feet (400 m).

A Great Wall

Emperor Qin Shi Huang started construction of the Great Wall of China around 214 BCE. Designed to protect China from northern invaders, the wall was one of the most ambitious military engineering projects in history. Workers began by connecting a series of existing walls in the northern part of China. They also built watchtowers along the wall. The towers allowed soldiers to watch for invaders.

The Great Wall of China was originally built to protect China from northern invaders. The wall was built over the course of many centuries and has become a major international tourist site. About ten million people visit the wall each year.

Ancient Guide to Warfare

Around 500 BCE, a Chinese general named Sun Tzu wrote a book about military strategy. Called *The Art of War*, it was the first known military manual. The book includes chapters on fighting on difficult terrain, attacking the enemy, and using spies. It is one of the most famous books on military strategy ever written. Thousands of copies are still sold around the world.

The wall stood 20 to 30 feet (6 to 9 m) high. It had a road on top, wide enough for five horses to ride side by side. If an enemy attacked, Chinese army units could quickly move along the wall and counterattack. Army units camped at the base of the wall. They signaled one another with fires built on top. Later emperors expanded the Great Wall. It eventually stretched about 4,500 miles (7,240 km) east to west across northern China.

Clay Warriors

In 1974 farmers in Xi'an, China, made an astounding discovery. When digging a well, they found a giant underground pit. The pit contained thousands of life-sized and half-sized human figures. They were made from clay heated so that it hardens into a material called terra-cotta.

The farmers had discovered the tomb of Qin Shi Huang. The figures were placed on the grave to guard Qin Shi Huang after death.

The tomb of ancient Chinese emperor Qin Shi Huang (259–210 BCE) contains thousands of terra-cotta soldiers. The terra-cotta army was created to guard the emperor in the afterlife.

Eventually, archaeologists found nearly eight thousand figures in several different pits. The figures are incredibly detailed. Their clothing and armor look just like the real thing. Even the soles of their shoes are adorned with tread patterns. The warriors include different kinds of soldiers: foot soldiers, charioteers, cavalry, crossbow archers, and officers. They stand in formation, as if prepared for battle. By studying the figures, archaeologists have learned about Chinese military clothing and operations during the time of Qin Shi Huang.

Martial Arts

The martial arts are ancient Asian combat and self-defense techniques. The earliest form of martial arts, kung fu, developed in China in the 1500s BCE. In kung fu, unarmed fighters use their hands and feet to strike or kick their opponents. In ancient China, warriors used kung fu against enemies. The ancient Chinese also used kung fu as physical and spiritual exercise.

Over the following centuries, Asian people developed many more types of martial arts. Around the world, many modern people practice martial arts for both exercise and self-defense.

CHAPTER FIVE

Ancient India

India's first civilization, the Indus Valley Civilization, flourished from about 2500 to 1700 BCE. A few hundred years later, people from central Asia took control of India. This group developed a complex culture. They also established two major religions: Buddhism and Hinduism. They created a rich body of art and literature, much of it based on Hindu teaching. Ancient Indian craftspeople produced elaborate jewelry and fabrics. Ancient India was also famous for its spices, including pepper, ginger, and cardamom.

In its early years, ancient India didn't have one central government. The territory was made up of many small kingdoms. That started to change in the 500s BCE. The kingdom of Magadha, in northeastern India, began to conquer other groups. By the 300s BCE, Magadha controlled much of central India.

A man named Chandragupta Maurya had bigger ambitions. He overthrew the Magadha ruler in the 320s BCE. He then conquered most of modern-day India,

37

Mohenjo-daro, built around 2600 BCE, was one of the largest settlements of the Indus Valley Civilization. The ruins, discovered in 1922, are located in modern-day Pakistan. Over time, kingdoms in this part of the world expanded by conquering other peoples through warfare.

Bangladesh, and Pakistan. His empire stretched across the Indian subcontinent, from the Bay of Bengal to the Arabian Sea. It grew rich from trade with China and the Middle East.

Change of Heart

Chandragupta's son Bindusara expanded the Mauryan Empire.

Arthashastra

Historians don't know much about Chandragupta, but they know that during his reign, one of his ministers named Chanakya wrote the *Arthashastra*. The book is a manual on how to run a country. It offers advice on foreign relations, government organization, warfare, law enforcement, economics, and politics.

Bindusara's son Ashoka expanded it even more. In 261 BCE, Ashoka conquered Kalinga, a region in eastern India. The fighting killed more than one hundred thousand people and wounded and displaced many times more.

When Ashoka realized how much suffering the conquest had caused, he was horrified and filled with regret. He renounced war and devoted the rest of his life to Buddhism.

War Elephants

The ancient Indians used many of the same military technologies as other ancient peoples. This technology included bows and arrows, spears, horses, and chariots. But the ancient Indians had something extra. They used elephants in battle. Elephants were bigger and more powerful than anything else on the ancient battlefield. The ancient Indians marched the animals into battle by the hundreds and sometimes the thousands.

Elephants were versatile military equipment. They could transport soldiers and supplies between battle sites. On the battlefield, they were most often used to charge at the enemy.

This modern drawing shows a war elephant on the battlefield. Armies used male elephants instead of females because the males were faster and more aggressive. War elephants charged enemy lines, trampled enemy soldiers, and caused enemy horses to stampede.

An elephant charge usually sent enemy soldiers running for their lives. Those who couldn't get out of the way fast enough were trampled. Elephants also terrified enemy horses, which often panicked. The horses reared up, threw off the rider and ran away.

Soldiers rode on the backs of elephants from big platforms called howdahs. Sometimes several archers rode on a howdah. From this perch, the archers had a superb view of the battlefield and their enemy targets. Sometimes generals rode in howdahs and commanded their soldiers from there.

Elephants have thick hides, which were not easily pierced by ancient weapons. Still, a fast-moving arrow or spear could injure an elephant. So ancient Indians sometimes outfitted the animals with metal armor, which protected their bodies and legs.

War elephants were unpredictable. When injured or frightened, they often trampled their own armies. Mahouts, or elephant handlers, sometimes had to kill elephants that went out of control. It took an extra-heavy arrow or a sharp spike to kill a war elephant.

The ancient Persians learned about war elephants from fighting the ancient Indians. The Persians used their own war elephants in 331 BCE against Alexander the Great, a famous Greek general. But even elephants could not stop Alexander's conquest of Persia. Soon elephants became standard military equipment in ancient Europe and the Middle East. One general, Hannibal, marched elephants over the Alps—the largest mountains in Europe—during a war against ancient Rome.

CHAPTER SIX

The Ancient Americas

A ncient America was home to thousands of different cultures. People lived in the far north, near the North Pole, all the way down to the southernmost tip of South America. Some ancient Americans were hunter-gatherers. Others were farmers or city dwellers.

Each group also had its own approach to warfare. Some ancient Americans rarely fought with outsiders. Other groups were more warlike. They fought to acquire new territory and resources. They took prisoners of war. In Central and South America, several large empires emerged. These empires amassed large armies to defend their territory, conquer new territory, and control conquered peoples.

Northern Warriors

Ancient North America did not have empires. Most ancient North Americans lived in small bands, ranging from a few dozen to several hundred people. Most were hunter-gatherers, although some were farmers. Indigenous American nations usually had

The Maya civilization thrived in Mesoamerica (central Mexico and Central America) from about 1000 BCE to 900 CE. They built sophisticated cities throughout the region, including Palenque (*above*) in what is now the Mexican state of Chiapas. Life at Palenque included warfare, through which the settlement aimed to maintain and extend its control of people, resources, and land in the area.

chiefs, and men of the tribe served as warriors when necessary. But tribes did not have permanent armies.

Occasionally, ancient North Americans clashed over food, water, or territory. Different tribes sometimes made alliances with one another to fight common enemies. Certain tribes were more warlike than others. The Navajo and the Apache, who lived in what is now the southwestern United States, often raided nearby Pueblo peoples. Indigenous peoples of the Great Plains held warriors in high regard. Plains warriors wore eagle feathers in their hair to mark the killing of enemies.

Like hunter-gatherers in other parts of the world, ancient North Americans fought with spears, clubs, and bows and arrows. In eastern North America, people sometimes fought with tomahawks. The tomahawk is similar to an ax. It had a sharp stone blade attached to a wooden handle. Warriors used tomahawks in two ways. Sometimes they struck an enemy with a tomahawk. Other times they threw it at the enemy.

Peoples of Middle America

Ancient Mexico and Central America made up a region called Mesoamerica. This region was home to a series of ancient cultures, including the Olmecs, the Maya, the Toltecs, and the Aztecs. Ancient Mesoamericans constructed temples and monuments, had large standing armies, and built big cities.

Maya culture flourished in Mesoamerica from about 1000 BCE to 900 CE. Archaeologists believe that war was common among the Maya. Maya cities were surrounded by high walls and deep ditches for defense against attackers. A mural in the ancient Maya city of Bonampak (in modern-day Mexico) shows Maya warriors beheading prisoners of war. Ancient Mayan hieroglyphics tell of wars between rival cities.

The spear was the Maya warrior's standard weapon. Maya wall paintings show warriors holding spears, although they also used clubs, battle-axes, and knives. The Maya used obsidian, a glasslike volcanic rock, to make spear tips, axes, knives, and other sharp tools. Weapons with obsidian blades

This section of a mural at the ancient Mayan city of Bonampak (in what is now the Mexican state of Chiapas) shows Maya warriors, armed with spears, and their seated prisoners. The Maya style of battle was largely hand to hand, with up-close thrusting and jabbing.

and points were razor sharp and deadly.

Aztec Empire

Maya society declined around 900 CE. After that the Toltec Empire emerged in Mesoamerica. It lasted for about three hundred years. The next superpower in the region was the Aztec Empire. It emerged in the 1400s and came to dominate Mesoamerica.

The Aztecs had a large army and government. The

45

The Florentine Codex of the mid-1500s shows Aztecs preparing for a feast to the sun. The figures in this panel hold *macuahuitls*, wooden swordlike weapons embedded with sharp blades of obsidian (a volcanic glass).

government was headed by an emperor and based in the city of Tenochtitlán. This enormous urban center was home to more than two hundred thousand people.

The Aztecs waged war to conquer surrounding territory as well as to take captives. In bloody ceremonies, they sacrificed prisoners of war to their gods. The Aztec warrior's primary weapon was the *macuahuitl*. This wooden club was lined with sharp pieces of obsidian. Warriors also fought with spears and bows and arrows.

Like other ancient peoples, Aztec warriors used spear-throwers to make their spears travel farther. Called an atlatl, the Aztec spear-thrower was made from a narrow piece of wood

Ancient Bioweapons

Biological weapons may seem like a modern invention. But they have been used for thousands of years. Bioweapons use bacteria, viruses, or other harmful material from living things. Ancient peoples used many bioweapons. They smeared feces on the tips of spears. The germs caused infections in the wounds. The bodies of people who died from infections diseases also became bioweapons. Soldiers put the bodies in catapults and hurled them into enemy camps or dumped them into an enemy's wells. This spread disease among the enemy army.

Poisonous arrows were a favorite bioweapon around the ancient world—from Asia to Europe to the Americas. In the Amazon River region in South America, for instance, ancient peoples coated arrow tips with curare, a poisonous plant extract. Amazonian warriors also used secretions from poison dart frogs. Warriors in ancient North America also coated their arrows with poisons.

or an animal bone. The spear sat in a groove cut into the top of the device. A hook or a loop of leather held the spear in place. Using an atlatl accurately took practice. It took a movement of the arm and wrist similar to cracking a whip or casting a fishing line. The thrower raised the atlatl overhead and then snapped their throwing arm forward. With an atlatl, a skilled warrior could hurl a spear at more than 100 miles (160 km) per hour.

Aztec warriors wore armor made from thick layers of cotton fabric. This armor offered some protection against spears and arrows. For better protection, the Aztecs sometimes soaked their armor in salty water. When the water dried, it left a hard, salty crust on the fabric, making it harder to cut. Aztec warriors also carried round shields into battle. The shields were made of leather and decorated with colored feathers.

CHAPTER SEVEN
Ancient Greece

A ncient Greece is remembered for its great philosophers, playwrights, and scientists. But it is also known for its military achievements. During the 400s BCE, Greek forces defeated the powerful Persian army twice. In the 300s BCE, under the leadership of Alexander the Great, Greece amassed a vast empire. Alexander's forces conquered Persia, Egypt, and parts of central Asia. Greek soldiers used the most advanced weapons of their day, and Greek generals developed shrewd battle tactics.

City-States at War

In its early years, around 800 BCE, ancient Greece was made up of city-states. These political units consisted of a city and the surrounding villages and farms. Each city-state operated like a separate country. It had its own laws, leaders, and army.

Athens and Sparta were the most powerful Greek city-states. They fought each other during the Peloponnesian War (431–404 BCE). During this conflict, soldiers used reliable

49

This mosaic shows a battle between Alexander the Great (*left, on horseback*), ruler of the Greek Empire, and Darius III (*center*) of the Persian Empire, in 333 BCE. The mosaic was made in the second century BCE and comes from the ancient Roman town of Pompeii.

weapons such as bows and arrows and spears.

In 424 BCE, the Spartans brought a new weapon to the battlefield. It was an early version of a flamethrower. The Spartans directed their flamethrower at the wooden walls of Delium, an enemy city. Sparta conquered Delium, and after many more years of fighting, Sparta finally defeated Athens. Thirty-three years later, the Greek city-state of Thebes conquered Sparta.

Research and Development

The ancient Greeks established colonies around the

Mediterranean Sea. One of these colonies was Syracuse, an island just south of Italy. Dionysius the Elder ruled Syracuse from 405 to 367 BCE. He desperately needed new weapons to protect Syracuse from Carthage, a colony on the coast of northern Africa.

Dionysius wanted a bow that could shoot heavier arrows than handheld bows. He brought engineers and craftspeople to Syracuse to develop the weapon. He organized them into teams—much like modern research and development (R&D) teams. Each team

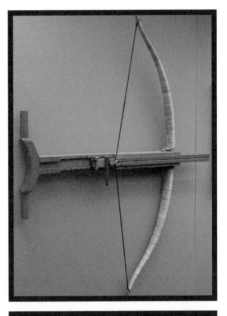

Archers braced the gastraphetes (a type of handheld crossbow) against their stomachs. The archer operated the bowstring with a sliding device in the middle of the shaft.

had one job and had to complete it on a strict deadline.

Dionysius's researchers invented the *gastraphetes*, or belly bow. The bow was bigger and more powerful than an ordinary bow. It was mounted on a central shaft. Archers braced the shaft against their stomachs while pulling the bowstring with both arms. The big bow could shoot a heavy arrow about 990 feet (300 m).

The belly bow was just the start. Greek craftspeople soon developed a belly bow that shot even larger arrows. The bow was too big and heavy for one archer to hold. Instead, it sat on a wooden base. To pull the bowstring, the archer turned a crank. Each turn of the crank pulled the bowstring back farther and farther, until the bow was ready for firing.

A Conqueror from the North

Fighting between city-states weakened ancient Greece. Macedonia was a kingdom north of Greece. Its king, Philip II, wanted to expand his territory. He reorganized and enlarged Macedonia's armed forces. Athens and Thebes united to fight Philip, but he quickly defeated them at the Battle of Chaeronea in 338 BCE. Greece became part of the Macedonian kingdom.

One of Philip's most powerful tools was the phalanx. In this infantry formation, soldiers stood shoulder to shoulder and lined up several rows deep. The whole block of soldiers advanced on an enemy as a unit.

Philip's phalanxes were twenty-eight rows deep. The front four rows had 1,024 soldiers armed with bows, spears, and slings. The next sixteen rows had 4,096 additional soldiers. Those at the front carried spears more than 13 feet (4 m) long. Behind them were soldiers armed with short swords, used for thrusting at close range. Eight lines containing 2,048 soldiers protected the rear of the phalanx. These soldiers carried swords, spears, slings, and other weapons. Each side of the phalanx was protected by cavalry soldiers. Philip sometimes combined several phalanxes into a grand phalanx, with up to thirty-two thousand soldiers.

At the start of a battle, Philip would order a cavalry charge to break up the enemy ranks. Next, he ordered the phalanx to charge. The soldiers ran at top speed, staying in formation. The enemy first faced short spears, arrows, and stones. Then came longer spears, and finally thousands of soldiers slashing with swords. It must have been terrifying.

The Katapultos

Military engineers kept improving on the gastraphetes. During Philip's campaigns, his engineers created large machines that could hurl not only arrows but also large stones. The Greeks called these devices *katapultos*. In English they are called catapults.

Ancient catapults were mounted on big wooden frames. A wooden beam held a stone or other ammunition. The beam was attached to twisted bands made of horsehair, animal tendon, or another stretchy material. The twisted bands stored up energy. When the bands untwisted, they transferred their energy to the beam. It sprang forward and hurled the ammunition through the air.

Catapults revolutionized ancient warfare. An attacking army might mount catapults on tall towers just outside an enemy city. The catapult operators would pummel the city walls with stones or other missiles. The attackers concentrated their firepower on one area of the walls and broke through quickly. In about 200 BCE, a Greek engineer wrote that city walls needed to be at least 15 feet (4.5 m) thick to withstand stones shot from catapults.

"It is the people who row the ships who give the city [Athens] its power, together with the helmsmen and the rowing masters and . . . officers and the shipwrights [shipbuilders]."

—Pseudo-Xenophon (the Old Oligarch), a Greek writer, circa 425 BCE

War at Sea

The mainland of Greece is bordered by water on three sides. It sits on a peninsula that juts into the Mediterranean Sea. It's no wonder, then, that the ancient Greeks were skilled shipbuilders. Greek merchant ships sailed the Mediterranean and nearby seas. The Greeks also developed some of the ancient world's best warships.

The earliest Greek warship was the bireme. Biremes had two rows of oars on each side, one on the ship's upper level and the other on the lower level. The placement was staggered, so that oars weren't positioned directly on top of one another and wouldn't crash into one another. The bireme had a single mast and a sail. Sailors removed the mast during battle. Some biremes were more than 80 feet (24 m) long.

Around 500 BCE, the Greeks began to use triremes. These warships had three rows of oars on each side. The typical ship was about 125 feet (38 m) long and 20 feet (6 m) wide. Trireme crews included about 160 rowers, along with dozens of heavily armed soldiers. The rowers propelled the ship at a peak speed of about 8 miles (13 km) per hour.

The Carthaginians, Syracusans, Egyptians, and other ancient peoples also built triremes. Fleets of triremes sailed in formation. When attacking, a group of triremes would maneuver into two columns. Each ship was protected on one side by another ship. The opposite side of the ship was exposed, so the crew could shoot arrows and hurl spears from that side.

Full Speed Ahead

Both biremes and triremes had wooden or metal beaks, or rams, on the front. The beak extended about 10 feet (3 m) in front of the ship's bow. It sat right at the waterline. Sailors used it to smash the hulls of enemy ships.

In the early years of ancient Greek warfare, ships fought at close range. The captain of a bireme or trireme would steer a ship directly into an enemy vessel, ramming it and hoping to tear a hole in its hull. Right after ramming, soldiers from the attacking ship scampered onto the enemy's boat and fought with swords, daggers, and spears.

This situation changed with the invention of catapults. With catapults mounted on deck, ships no longer had to ram an enemy ship to damage it. Soldiers could just launch stones and other missiles from catapults from long distances.

To carry catapults, ancient navies needed bigger warships. The Greeks built the quinquereme, which was about 150 feet (45 m) long. It still had three levels of oars on each side. But two soldiers pulled each oar on the top two levels, and one soldier pulled each oar on the bottom level. Later warships were even bigger, with more room for catapults and more soldiers pulling oars.

Claws of Archimedes

Archimedes was a Greek engineer who lived in the 200s BCE. He studied physics and mathematics and also invented machines. Archimedes lived in Syracuse. He used his mechanical knowledge to create weapons for the Syracusan army.

Syracuse was a port city. Its walls stood next to the

sea, which made them vulnerable to attack by water. To defend the city against attacking ships, Archimedes created a machine called the Claws of Archimedes.

The claws looked like a modern construction crane. It had one upright beam with a horizontal beam on top. The upright beam stood inside the city walls. The horizontal beam projected out over the top of the walls, above the sea. A sharp, clawlike hook hung off the beam from the end of a rope. The other end of the rope, behind the city walls, was attached to a team of oxen.

When an enemy ship threatened, Syracusan soldiers readied the Claws of Archimedes. When the ship got near enough, soldiers lowered the hook toward the water and snagged the ship's hull with the pointed claw. Behind the city walls, the oxen then pulled the rope, lifting the ship out of the water.

"A Nasty Present"

Across the ancient world, most soldiers loaded their slings with stones. But the ancient Greeks devised a better missile for slinging. They made bullets by pouring molten lead into molds. The molds were about 1 inch (2.5 cm) across. Lead is denser than stone, so a lead bullet weighs more than a stone of the same size. Because of the extra weight, lead bullets shot from slings did more damage than stones. Molded lead bullets flew straighter and hit their targets with more accuracy. The Greeks sometimes etched insulting messages into the bullet molds. The messages were then imprinted on the bullets. One message said: "A Nasty Present."

CHAPTER EIGHT
Ancient Rome

A ncient Rome traces its beginnings to people called the Latins. Around 2000 BCE, they began grazing herds of sheep in central Italy. By 750 BCE, the Latins had settled into permanent farming villages. One village grew into the city of Rome.

The Romans conquered other groups on the Italian Peninsula. By 264 BCE, Rome ruled all of Italy. Rome fought against Carthage during the Punic Wars, a series of struggles between 264 and 146 BCE. During these wars, Rome conquered additional lands around the Mediterranean Sea, including Spain and Greece. By the second century CE, Rome controlled much of Europe, the Middle East, and northern Africa.

Maintaining an Empire

To defend its empire, ancient Rome built a strong army. The main military unit was the legion. During the reign of Emperor Augustus, from 27 BCE to 14 CE, Rome had almost thirty

57

The Appian Way (*above*) was a main route for transporting military supplies from ancient Rome to military bases in southern Italy. The first section of the road was completed in the early 300s BCE, and construction to extend the road continued into the 200s BCE.

legions. Each legion had six thousand soldiers. Legions were divided into smaller units called cohorts, each with four hundred soldiers. Cohorts were broken down into centuries, groups of one hundred soldiers. An officer called a centurion led each century. Soldiers usually enlisted in the Roman legions for twenty years.

To quickly transport troops and weapons, the Romans built more than 50,000 miles (80,500 km) of roads. These connected all parts of the vast empire. Roman roads were built to last. They had sturdy stone foundations up to 5 feet (1.5 m) deep. They were paved with blocks of cut stone.

Dressed for Battle

Military uniforms varied over the years of ancient Roman history. And different kinds of soldiers wore different kinds of uniforms. But the typical Roman foot soldier wore a belted, knee-length garment called a tunic. Soliders wore metal armor across their chest and stomach. They also wore shin armor and a metal helmet. A round or rectangular shield gave them additional protection from incoming stones, arrows, spears, and dagger thrusts.

The soldiers' combat boots were well designed for support, comfort, and protection. The boots looked like modern leather sandals. They were open-toed, with laces at the ankle. The upper portions of the boots were webbed, which allowed them to flex as soldiers marched. The openings in the leather also allowed the boots to dry quickly after marches in wet weather. The soles were made from single pieces of leather. Iron nails pounded into the soles acted like cleats on modern athletic shoes. The nails improved traction and helped reduce wear on the soles.

Roman Artillery

Roman legions used catapults for hurling stones, arrows, and other objects at enemies. The most powerful Roman catapult could hurl a 55-pound (25 kg) rock more than 1,320 feet (400 m).

But catapults were heavy and difficult to transport. They were not practical for the fast-paced action of battle. Just before the first century CE, the Roman army began using smaller, more mobile catapults. Each Roman legion traveled with about thirty small catapults. During the second and

This modern reenactment of ancient Roman warfare shows the testudo, or tortoise, formation.

third centuries CE, Roman engineers developed several new kinds of artillery. The *cheiroballista* was a small arrow thrower mounted on a wheeled carriage. The *manuballista* and the *arcuballista* were similar, but they had no carriages. They were handheld arrow shooters, similar to crossbows.

The Fighting Tortoise

When marching toward the enemy, the ancient Romans sometimes used a clever technique. Foot soldiers organized themselves into a formation called a testudo. The word is Latin for tortoise. The soldiers lined up in rows, three or more rows deep. The first row held their shields in front of them. The following rows held their shields above their heads. The soldiers on the ends of rows held their shields out to the side. The edges of the shields overlapped or had very little space between them. The formation was like a big metal box. Enemy stones, spears, and arrows would hit the shields and bounce off, rarely getting through to the soldiers inside.

Roman Britain

Roman general Julius Caesar invaded Britain in 55 BCE but was not able to conquer the territory. In 43 CE, Roman armies again invaded Britain and this time succeeded. Modern-day England and Wales became part of the Roman Empire.

The Romans built towns, temples, government offices, public baths, roads, and forts throughout their British territory. In the north, near the border with modern-day Scotland, Roman soldiers built Hadrian's Wall, named for the Roman emperor. The wall was designed to protect Roman Britain from the Scots and Picts, who lived farther north. It ran for 73 miles (117 km) across northern England.

Britain remained a Roman province for more than three hundred years. But as the Roman Empire declined in the 300s, Rome struggled to protect Britain from outside invaders. Finally, Roman troops left Britain to defend other parts of the empire. Scots and Picts then invaded Britain, followed by Angles, Saxons, and Jutes from the European mainland. By the end of the 500s, much of Britain was under Anglo-Saxon control.

Building Better Warships

Like other ancient peoples, the Romans sometimes fought at sea. They used triremes and quinqueremes, based on Greek designs. But the Romans also improved on the designs. Roman ships had thicker, stronger gunwales than did Greek ships. The gunwales could better withstand ramming by an enemy ship. Roman ships also had heavier, stronger beaks than did Greek ships. These beaks were better for smashing through the hulls of enemy vessels. Some Roman warships had fighting towers from which archers shot arrows at enemy sailors.

During the First Punic War (264–241 BCE), the Romans introduced a new device to warships. Called the *corvus*, it was a narrow wooden plank, about 18 feet (5 m) long. It had a heavy metal spike attached to one end. Before or after a fight, the corvus stood upright near the bow of the Roman warship. Ropes held it in place. But when an enemy warship got close enough, sailors let the corvus come crashing down. The spiked end hit the enemy deck. The spike dug into the deck and held tight. Then Roman sailors swarmed across the corvus and onto the enemy ship, where they fought with the enemy hand to hand.

Decline and Fall

Maintaining the enormous Roman Empire wasn't easy. Enemies were constantly attacking the edges of Roman territory. Germanic tribes attacked in the north. Parthian forces attacked from the east. At the same time, Roman nobility fought among themselves for the title of emperor of Rome. Some nobles seized power by force. Amid the political chaos, in the 200s

CE, Roman institutions began to break down. The Roman army steadily weakened. Its soldiers became less disciplined and less skillful.

In the 300s, the empire split into eastern and western halves. The Eastern Roman Empire set up a new capital in Turkey. The eastern empire grew larger and stronger and became known as the Byzantine Empire. But the Western Roman Empire continued to collapse.

Around 390, a wealthy Roman named Flavius Vegetius Renatus wrote a book about Roman military practices. Called *Concerning Military Matters*, this book described the Roman legions of earlier centuries. It discussed the training and discipline of soldiers, the organization of military units, the responsibilities of officers, and battle tactics and strategy. Vegetius said that the Roman Empire could restore its strength by returning to its earlier military glory.

But it was too late for ancient Rome. By the fifth century CE, the Roman army was stretched too thin to defend all parts of the empire. One Germanic group invaded Roman-held Spain and North Africa. Another attacked the city of Rome itself. Finally, in 476, the Germanic leader Odoacer captured Rome. This ended the Roman Empire.

CONCLUSION
After the Ancients

After Rome fell to invaders, Europe entered the Middle Ages (500–1500 CE). Many small kingdoms emerged in Europe during this era. Kings and other nobility amassed armies and fought one another for power and territory.

The Middle Ages are sometimes called the Dark Ages because few people kept written records then. Few Europeans went to school or could read or write. Few craftspeople knew about or improved upon ancient technology. But people of the Middle Ages didn't forget about ancient times. European kings were particularly interested in the warfare of ancient Rome. Scribes, or writers, made copies of Vegetius's *Concerning Military Matters*. Kings and other rulers studied the book to learn all they could about organizing their armies and outwitting their enemies.

Weapons in Europe did not change much during the early Middle Ages. Soldiers continued to fight with bows and arrows, catapults, and other weapons developed in ancient times. For protection against invaders, rulers built

An illustration from the book *Campaign in India 1857–1858* shows Indian soldiers mobilizing canons before battle. Bullets and cannonballs were far more powerful than arrows and other early missiles.

strong castles. These fortifications had high stone walls, watchtowers, drawbridges, moats, and other defensive features. Castles were homes for rulers and their families, headquarters for kingdoms, and bases of operations for military campaigns.

Bang, Bang

Midway through the Middle Ages, military technology changed dramatically. Around 900 CE, Chinese inventors learned to combine saltpeter, charcoal, and sulfur to make gunpowder. This explosive material can propel a bullet or a cannonball with great speed and force. The Chinese first used gunpowder in small cannons. The technology spread from China to the Middle East and then to Europe.

After cannons, military engineers applied gunpowder technology to handheld firearms, such as muskets and rifles. Warfare had always been deadly. But gunpowder made it even deadlier and more destructive. Cannonballs could knock down castle walls. Bullets shot from handheld firearms could pierce metal armor.

The Business of War

By the 1500s, Europe was home to large, powerful states. These included France, Britain, and Spain. Like the ancient empires before them, these nations needed strong armies and navies. Equipped with firearms and cannons, as well as more ancient technology such as horses, swords, and daggers, European soldiers battled one another. They also conquered territories in Asia, Africa, and the Americas.

In the 1700s and 1800s, the Industrial Revolution brought new machines, such as steam engines. People developed railroads and other transportation systems. The new technology wasn't created specifically for warfare. But people quickly realized that the new machines had great military benefits. For instance, trains could move an army in a few hours much farther than soldiers marching on foot could travel in days. And soldiers transported by train arrived at the battlefield rested and ready to fight.

In the early 1900s, officers could use telephones and radios to communicate with one another. They used gasoline-powered trucks to carry troops and equipment. They used airplanes to spy on and shoot at the enemy from above. Some new inventions were specifically made for the military. These included tanks, fighter planes, machine guns, and submarines.

World War

By World War I (1914–1918), warfare was becoming more mechanized. No one fought with bows and arrows anymore. Armies attacked the enemy with rifles, machine guns, tanks, and big artillery pieces.

In World War II (1939–1945) additional technology was introduced. One example is radar. This device uses radio waves to track moving or hard-to-see objects. During World War II, armies used radar to track enemy ships and planes.

The atomic bomb was the most destructive military technology ever used. The United States used this weapon at the end of World War II. It dropped atomic bombs on Hiroshima and Nagasaki, two Japanese cities, in 1945. The explosions destroyed the cities and killed tens of thousands of people. This was the only time atomic bombs have been used in war.

Modern Times

Modern warfare is completely different from warfare in ancient

A marine air traffic controller monitors radar. Radar equipment sends out pulses of radio waves, which bounce off any objects in their way. When the waves bounce back, they are picked up and turned into imagery that can be seen onscreen.

times. Digital technology and unpiloted drones give modern armies far more information than ancient armies ever had. Armies, navies, and air forces get second-by-second information about enemy positions via satellites. Some information comes from drones. These flying robots can be controlled remotely from miles away or programmed to fly themselves on a specific flight path. As they fly, drones may capture videos of targets and send them back to a control center. Some drones carry small bombs or missiles to attack enemy targets as well. Laser beams guide bombs and other missiles precisely to their targets.

A new form of warfare is taking place without guns or bombs. Cyber warfare involves the use of computer viruses and hacking to steal military secrets from other countries or even disrupt physical facilities that have an internet connection.

Does this mean that all ancient technology is no longer useful? Do we have nothing left to learn from ancient warriors? Modern military leaders would be quick to answer no. At the United States Military Academy, which trains US army officers, students still read Sun Tzu's *The Art of War.* They also study Vegetius's *Concerning Military Matters.* Modern officers find that much ancient military advice is still true many centuries later.

Many ancient tactics—such as guerrilla warfare and siege warfare—are still used in modern times. For instance, the modern US military trains soldiers to fight in small groups and to carry out quick ambushes, much as the ancient Scythians did thousands of years ago. Bioweapons modeled after those used in ancient times are still available, but most are banned by the international community.

Ancient War Machines Come to Life

People are still fascinated with ancient war machines. Modern engineers have reproduced ancient-style catapults according to the original plans. One reproduction catapult fired an arrow into a target and then fired another arrow that split the first one in two.

In the mid-1980s, British historians built a full-sized trireme based on ancient pictures and texts. Called the *Olympias*, the boat is 131 feet (40 m) long and 20 feet (6 m) wide. It has seats for 170 rowers, 85 per side, on three levels. It also has two sails. Project leaders tested the *Olympias* at sea six times between 1987 and 1994. Each time, organizers recruited 170 volunteers to pull on the oars. Everyone pulling together got the ship moving at a speed of 9 knots—a little faster than 10 miles (17 km) per hour. The ship also was very easy to maneuver.

The Lessons of War

War has changed the course of human history. By studying war, we can find out about the past. By studying ancient military technology, we can learn even more. Ancient warfare combines many other technologies, such as machinery, construction, communications, and transportation. Ancient warfare technology helps us understand ancient society as a whole. It helps explain how history affects the world today. Maybe knowledge about warfare through the ages and the terrible waste of human lives it causes will help prevent wars in the future, or even end it forever.

TIMELINE

ca. 5000 BCE People in the Middle East begin using copper to make tools and weapons.

ca. 3100 BCE Upper Egypt conquers Lower Egypt, and the two kingdoms unite.

ca. 3000 BCE People in the Middle East begin making tools and weapons from bronze. People in the Middle East start to use wheels in both transportation and warfare.

1500s BCE Kung fu develops in China.

ca. 1550 BCE Hittites invade Mesopotamia. They use iron weapons, which give them the advantage in battle.

ca. 1270 BCE Ramses II of Egypt and Hattusilis III, king of the Hittites, sign the earliest known peace treaty.

513 BCE The Persian emperor Darius I invades Scythian territory, but Scythian guerrilla attacks turn back his forces.

ca. 500 BCE. Sun Tzu writes *The Art of War*, the world's first military manual. The ancient Greeks begin using triremes in sea battles.

431–404 BCE The Greek city-states of Athens and Sparta fight each other during the Peloponnesian War.

ca. 400 BCE The ancient Chinese invent the crossbow. Greek engineers invent the gastraphetes.

338 BCE Philip of Macedonia defeats Athens and Thebes at the Battle of Chaeronea. Greece becomes part of Philip's empire.

320s BCE Chandragupta Maurya takes power in India.

200s BCE Archimedes designs war machines, including the Claws of Archimedes, for the Syracusan army.

264–146 BCE Rome and Carthage fight the Punic Wars.

261 BCE Indian emperor Ashoka conquers the territory of Kalinga and then renounces warfare.

ca. 214 BCE Emperor Qin Shi Huang begins construction on the Great Wall of China.

43 CE The Roman army successfully invades Britain.

300s	The Roman Empire splits into eastern and western halves.
ca. 390	Flavius Vegetius Renatus writes *Concerning Military Matters*.
476	The Germanic leader Odoacer captures the city of Rome, ending the Roman Empire.
900	People in China invent gunpowder.
1974	Farmers in Xi'an, China, discover Emperor Qin Shi Huang's tomb and thousands of terra-cotta warriors.
1987–1994	Historians test the *Olympias*, a reproduction of a Greek trireme, at sea.
2021	Researchers in Italy discover a fifteen-hundred-year-old Roman road on the ocean floor in Venice. The road led to an ancient dock.

GLOSSARY

ammunition: projectiles fired from guns and other weapons

archaeologist: a scientist who studies the remains of past human cultures

artifact: a human-made object, especially one characteristic of a certain group or historical period

artillery: weapons used for firing missiles at long range

bioweapon: a harmful biological agent (such as a pathogenic microorganism or a neurotoxin) used as a weapon to cause death or disease, usually on a large scale

catapult: an ancient mechanical device used for hurling large stones, arrows, and other missiles

cavalry: soldiers who fight on horseback

chariot: a two-wheeled, horse-drawn cart used in battle

drone: a flying robot controlled remotely or by program to gather intelligence or carry weapons

empire: a political unit made up of different nations or territories, held together and ruled by the strongest nation in the group

excavation: the process of digging underground, especially to look for artifacts

guerrilla warfare: ambushes, raids, and other tactics carried out by small, loosely organized bands of fighters

gunpowder: an explosive material used inside guns and to propel bullets, cannonballs, and other ammunition

gunwale: the upper rim around a boat or a ship

hafting: attaching the handle and the head of a tool or weapon

infantry: soldiers who fight on foot

missile: an object that is thrown by hand or shot from a weapon at a distant target

momentum: a property of a moving body that determines the length of time required to bring it to rest when under the action of a constant force

phalanx: troops organized into a rectangular formation, with lines of soldiers standing many rows deep

siege: an attack in which troops surround a city or fortification, firing upon defenders and inhabitants and cutting off their supply of food, water, and other provisions

strategy: an overall battle plan

tactics: an army's minute-by-minute movements

SOURCE NOTES

14   "If my lord . . . will assemble quickly." Robert Drews, *The End of the Bronze Age: Changes in Warfare and the Catastrophe ca. 1200 B.C.* (Princeton, NJ: Princeton University Press, 1993), 150.

48   "A very severe . . . with their slings." Bernal Díaz del Castillo, "The Memoirs of the Conquistador Bernal Díaz del Castillo," Project Gutenberg, 2010, accessed May 17, 2023, http://www.gutenberg.org/cache/epub/32475/pg32475.txt.

53   "It is the . . . and the shipwrights." Brian Fagan, ed., *The Seventy Great Inventions of the Ancient World* (London: Thames and Hudson, 2004), 200.

56   "A Nasty Present." Anthony M. Snodgrass, *Arms and Armor of the Greeks* (Baltimore: Johns Hopkins University Press, 1999), 117.

59   "Veni, vidi, vici." Merriam-Webster, *Webster's New Biographical Dictionary* (Springfield, MA: Merriam-Webster, 1988), 792.

SELECTED BIBLIOGRAPHY

Dupuy, R. Ernest, and Trevor N. Dupuy. *The Encyclopedia of Military History from 3500 B.C. to the Present*. 2nd rev. ed. New York: Harper and Row, 1986.

Fagan, Brian M. *Kingdoms of Gold, Kingdoms of Jade: The Americas before Columbus*. London: Thames and Hudson, 1991.

———., ed. *Discovery! Unearthing the New Treasures of Archaeology*. London: Thames and Hudson, 2007.

———. *The Seventy Great Inventions of the Ancient World*. London: Thames and Hudson, 2004.

Hackett, John, ed. *Warfare in the Ancient World*. New York: Facts on File, 1989.

James, Peter, and Nick Thorpe. *Ancient Inventions*. New York: Ballantine Books, 1994.

Keay, John. *India: A History*. New York: Grove Press, 2010.

Keegan, John. *A History of Warfare*. New York: Vintage Books, 1993.

Kopper, Philip. *The Smithsonian Book of North American Indians: Before the Coming of the Europeans*. Washington, DC: Smithsonian Books, 1986.

O'Connell, Robert L. *Of Arms and Men: A History of War, Weapons, and Aggression*. New York: Oxford University Press, 1989.

Roberts, J. M. *The New Penguin History of the World*. 5th ed. London: Penguin Books, 2002.

Robertshaw, Andrew. *A Soldier's Life: A Visual History of Soldiers through the Ages*. New York: Lodestar Books, 1997.

FURTHER READING

Books

Miller, Michael. *Cyberspies*. Minneapolis: Twenty-First Century Books, 2021.
> War is no longer only waged on the battlefield. Every day, hackers try to break into databases of companies and governments to get information and disrupt operations. This book takes a behind-the-scenes look at the new frontier of warfare, cyberspying.

Snow, Peter, ed. *Battles Map by Map*. New York: DK Penguin Random House, 2021.
> Throughout the course of human civilizations, certain battles have changed the course of history. From the ancient world to World War II, this book takes a visual tour of the greatest battles in history through historic maps, paintings, and objects from the battlefield.

Woods, Michael, and Mary B. Woods. *Machines through the Ages*. Minneapolis: Twenty-First Century Books, 2024.
> With only six simple machines, humans have made countless innovations to help them tell time, build monuments and pyramids, and even change their landscape. Explore the science behind such machines as the Chinese wooden ox (wheelbarrow), knives used in ancient brain surgeries, and the deadly Claws of Archimedes.

Wyse, Elizabeth. *A History of the Classical World*. London: Arcturus, 2021.
> Greece and Rome both controlled vast empires in the ancient world. This illustrated book explores the history of the rise of both empires, along with information about their architecture, art, and politics.

Xavier, Clément, and Lisa Lugrin. *The Bodyguard Unit: Edith Garrud, Women's Suffrage, and Jujitsu*. Minneapolis: Graphic Universe, 2023.
> When women began demanding the right to vote, they often faced violence. To defend themselves, the Women's Social and Political Union formed an all-woman security unit. This graphic retelling follows the life of Edith Garrud, a pioneering suffragette and instructor in women's self-defense.

Websites

Ancient Greece
  https://education.nationalgeographic.org/resource/resource
  -library-ancient-greece/
  This National Geographic explores ancient Greek history
  and culture. Learn about how ancient sailors explored the
  Mediterranean and how Alexander the Great ruled one of the
  largest empires in history.

Catapults
  https://segedunumromanfort.org.uk/catapults
  The Roman Fort of Segedunum is the most excavated fort along
  Hadrian's Wall. This web page run by the Segedunum museum
  explores the many ballistic weapons used by the Romans, such as
  the ballista and the onager.

The Chariot in Egyptian Warfare
  http://www.touregypt.net/featurestories/chariots.htm
  This tourism website offers a well-researched article about
  Egyptian war chariots.

Pipe Tomahawk Presented to Chief Tecumseh
  https://americanindian.si.edu/exhibitions/infinityofnations
  /woodlands/176249.html
  Learn about the history of pipe tomahawks as symbols of peace
  and war between European colonists and Indigenous Americans
  through this article by the Smithsonian Institute.

The Trireme Trust
  http://www.triremetrust.org.uk/
  Here you'll learn about the *Olympias*, a reproduction Greek trireme
  built in the 1980s. The site explains the building project and tells
  how the *Olympias* performed at sea.

INDEX

ABOUT THE AUTHORS

Michael Woods is a science and medical journalist in Washington, DC. He has won many national writing awards. Mary B. Woods is a school librarian. Their past books include the fifteen–volume *Disasters Up Close* series and many titles in the *Seven Wonders* series. The Woodses have four children. When not writing, reading, or enjoying their seven grandchildren, the Woodses travel to gather material for future books.

PHOTO ACKNOWLEDGMENTS